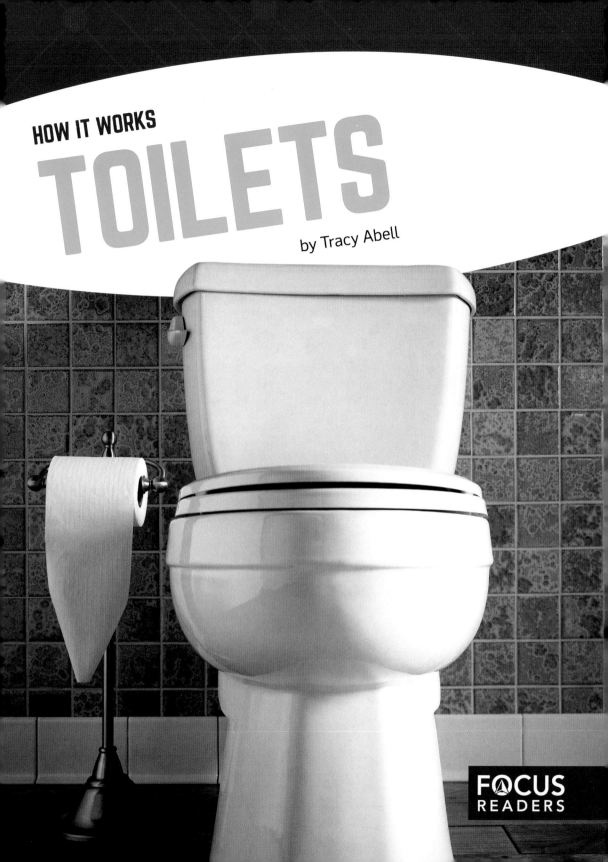

HOW IT WORKS
TOILETS

by Tracy Abell

FOCUS
READERS

FOCUS READERS

WWW.FOCUSREADERS.COM

Focus Readers is distributed by North Star Editions:
sales@northstareditions.com | 888-417-0195

Produced for Focus Readers by Red Line Editorial.

Content Consultant: Daniel Gerling, Assistant Professor, English Department, Augustana University

Photographs ©: Miles Sherrill/iStockphoto, cover, 1; Benedictus/Shutterstock Images, 4–5; Anton Ermachkov/Shutterstock Images, 7; Allkindza/iStockphoto, 9; Africa Studio/Shutterstock Images, 10–11; Rasulovs/iStockphoto, 13; Designua/Shutterstock Images, 14; NWStock/Shutterstock Images, 16–17; *Popular Science Monthly* Volume 33, 18; Jevtic/iStockphoto, 21; ZCHE/New Frontier Tiny Homes/Wenn/Newscom, 23; Somsak Suwanput/Shutterstock Images, 24–25; vichinterlang/iStockphoto, 27; yampi/Shutterstock Images, 29

ISBN
978-1-63517-238-6 (hardcover)
978-1-63517-303-1 (paperback)
978-1-63517-433-5 (ebook pdf)
978-1-63517-368-0 (hosted ebook)

Library of Congress Control Number: 2017935933

Printed in the United States of America
Mankato, MN
June, 2017

ABOUT THE AUTHOR

Tracy Abell lives in the Rocky Mountain foothills where she enjoys running on the trails. She often sees coyotes, foxes, rabbits, magpies, and meadowlarks out there in the open space. She sometimes wishes she'd see a toilet.

TABLE OF CONTENTS

CHAPTER 1

THE HISTORY OF TOILETS

Before the invention of toilets, people used benches with seat holes above open pits. Some benches had only one hole. Other benches had up to 20. People also used **chamber pots**. In some ancient cities, people had sewer systems to deal with waste. But in other places, they simply dug holes in the ground.

The ancient Romans built this public bathroom in Ostia Antica, Italy.

Many castles in Europe had garderobes. These tiny rooms were on the castles' outside walls. They contained a bench with a hole above a narrow shaft. Waste dropped down the shaft to a sewer or a vault. Sometimes it went right into the castle's moat or onto the bare ground.

Sir John Harington designed the first flush toilet in 1596. It had a pan with a seat to sit on. A tank held water above the pan. When the handle was pushed, water

CRITICAL THINKING

What are some improvements that a toilet offers compared to a chamber pot?

This toilet was built into the walls of Gravensteen Castle in Ghent, Belgium.

flowed down a pipe and into the pan.
The water flushed out the pan into an
underground sewage tank.

Harington's invention did not become common for another 200 years. One reason was that odors still came back up the pipe. This made the home smell bad. People also thought that the odors coming from the pipes could spread disease.

A later inventor, Alexander Cummings, designed the S-trap. The S-trap was a bend in the pipe. It kept bad smells from coming back up.

By the end of the 1700s, flush toilets had become more common in Europe. But the rest of the world still used other methods. Inventors continued to make improvements. Between 1900 and 1932,

Before Harington's invention became common, many people still used chamber pots.

inventors in the United States created more than 350 toilet designs. One of those designs was for a toilet with a **siphon**. This design became the type of toilet we use today.

CHAPTER 2

FLAPPERS, FLOATS, AND FLUSHING

A toilet's tank holds water. Inside the tank, a part called the flapper covers the tank's drain hole. The flapper is hollow and filled with air. In some toilets, a lift chain connects the flapper to the toilet's flush handle. Pushing down on the handle causes the chain to move. This lifts the flapper.

A plumber fixes the pipe that brings water to the toilet's tank.

Other toilets use linked rods to lift the flapper. These are called lift rods.

Lifting the flapper uncovers the drain hole. Water flows out of the tank and into the toilet's bowl. Once the toilet has finished flushing, the flapper moves back down to cover the drain hole. When the flapper is in the closed position, no more water can leave the tank.

Next, the toilet's tank must be refilled. The fill valve opens. This valve controls how much water is let into the tank.

CRITICAL THINKING

What would happen if a toilet's lift chain broke?

Some toilets have a button on top instead of a flush handle.

When the fill valve is open, water from the pipes can flow into the tank. A part

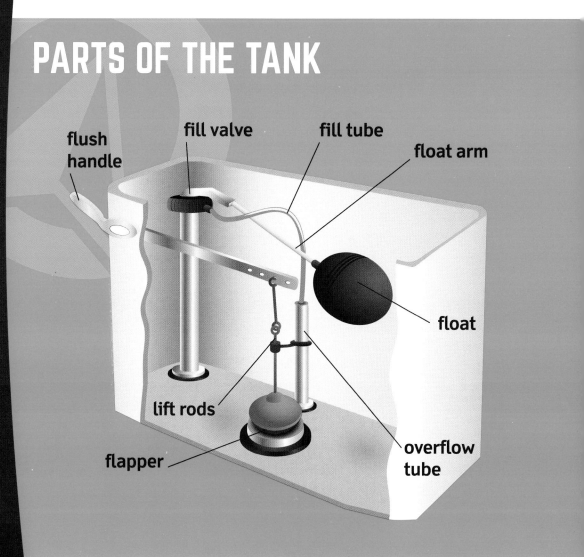

PARTS OF THE TANK

flush handle

fill valve

fill tube

float arm

float

lift rods

overflow tube

flapper

called the float arm opens and closes the fill valve. The float arm is connected to a float. The float sits on top of the water in the tank. As the water inside the tank goes down, the float moves down, too. This pulls the float arm down and causes the fill valve to open.

Water from the fill tube flows through the open fill valve. It refills the tank. As the water level in the tank rises, the float moves up, too. When the tank is full, the fill valve closes. As long as the water holds the float in place, the fill valve will stay closed. No more water can enter the tank from the pipes.

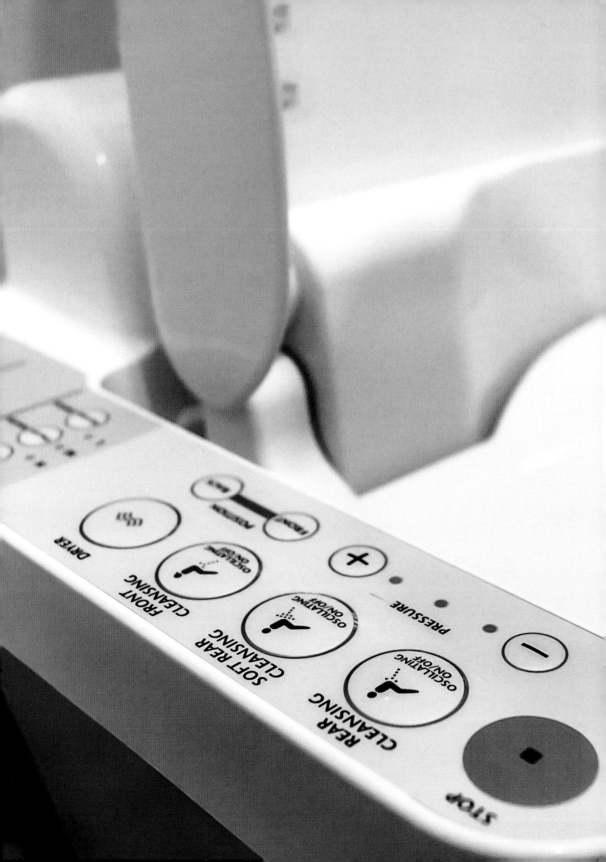

CHAPTER 3

FROM SIPHON TO SEWER

When a toilet is flushed, water flows from the tank to the bowl. Some of the water enters the bowl through holes in the bowl's rim. These holes are slanted. The slant causes the water to enter the bowl at an angle. This makes the water swirl around the bowl. The swirling motion helps clean the toilet.

Toilet bowls with bidet seats can also spray water for personal cleaning.

Water also enters the bowl through the siphon jet. The siphon jet is a small hole near the bottom of the bowl.

The trap is a curved part of a toilet's pipe. It holds water. The trap helps keep

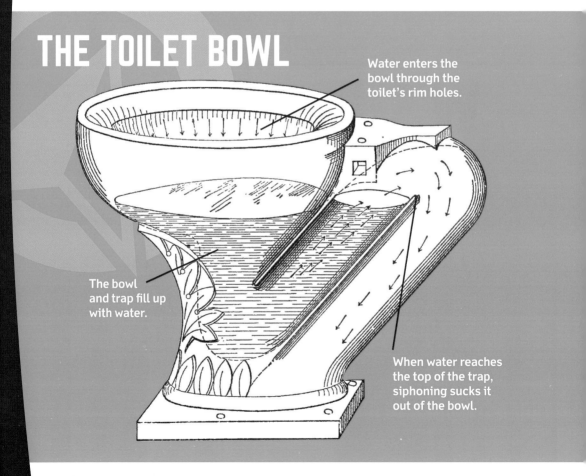

THE TOILET BOWL

Water enters the bowl through the toilet's rim holes.

The bowl and trap fill up with water.

When water reaches the top of the trap, siphoning sucks it out of the bowl.

the right amount of water in the bowl. It also prevents sewer odors from coming up through the pipe.

As soon as the bowl's water level reaches the top of the trap, **siphoning** sucks everything from the bowl. The water and waste go up and over the trap. Then they are sent out to the sewer pipes.

Siphoning stops when there is no longer enough water in the bowl to reach the top of the trap. The water that has not yet spilled over the top of the trap flows back into the bowl. A tube in the tank sends clean water to the bowl as well. The water level rises until the trap is refilled.

When the correct amount of water is in the bowl, the toilet is ready for the next flush.

Toilets need strong water movement for flushing. Minerals from the water can build up in toilets. They can clog the rim holes and siphon jet. This makes it harder for water to pass through the holes and the siphon jet.

A toilet with mineral buildup will not flush as well. It must be flushed more often. This wastes water. Plumbers suggest cleaning the rim holes and siphon to keep a strong flush.

It is important to clean a toilet's bowl regularly.

COMPOSTING TOILET

Composting toilets are not connected to a sewer system. Instead, waste begins to transform to compost while inside the toilet. Human waste is mostly liquid. Composting toilets use vents to help this liquid **evaporate**. Solid waste is broken down in the composting chamber. This chamber uses bacteria to turn the waste into compost. The bacteria need a mixture of oxygen, moisture, and heat.

Some composting toilets have a handle for turning the chamber. This helps oxygen move through the waste. It speeds up the composting process. Adding sawdust or peat moss can also speed up the process and help stop odors.

It takes 6 to 12 months for waste to turn into safe compost. As the waste breaks down, it drops

Composting toilets do not use any water at all.

onto a tray. The tray can be removed when the compost is ready to be used. The compost makes excellent fertilizer. It can be added to soil under trees and bushes. Sometimes it is used to grow vegetables!

CHAPTER 4

DESIGNING BETTER BATHROOMS

Flush toilets make people's lives much easier. But not everyone has access to toilets. The World Health Organization (WHO) studies **sanitation** around the world. It collects information about waste disposal and health. According to the WHO, only 54 percent of people had toilets or **latrines** in 1990.

This temporary toilet was set up in a jungle.

By 2015, that number had increased to 68 percent of people. However, 2.4 billion people still lacked basic sanitation **facilities**. Poor sanitation can lead to disease and even death. Better sanitation can lead to improved health. It has other benefits, too. For example, students with access to clean and safe toilet facilities are more likely to finish their educations.

The United Nations (UN) believes everyone should have access to

CRITICAL THINKING

Why might having access to clean toilet facilities make it more likely for children to finish school?

Sustainable Organic Integrated Livelihoods (SOIL) provides many families in Haiti with composting toilets.

sanitation. The UN wants countries around the world to work together to make that happen.

People are also working to design toilets that use less water. In the United States, the average family of four uses 400 gallons (1,514 L) of water each day. Approximately 27 percent of that water is used to flush toilets.

Most modern toilets use 1.6 gallons (6.1 L) of water per flush. That is less than half the water used in older toilets. But people are still working to create better designs.

Some toilets use a dual-flush system. Instead of a flush handle, these toilets have two flush buttons. One button is for a full flush. This flush is for solids. The other button is for flushing liquids. This flush uses two-thirds of the amount of water that a full flush uses.

Regular toilets can be converted into dual-flush toilets. Hardware stores sell kits. They include buttons that replace the toilet's flush handle.

This dual-flush toilet has its two flush buttons mounted on the wall behind it.

Another new toilet design also helps **conserve** water. It uses only 1.3 gallons (4.9 L) of water per flush. Replacing every old toilet in the United States with this new design could save 520 billion gallons (2 trillion L) of water each year.

FOCUS ON
TOILETS

Write your answers on a separate piece of paper.

1. Write a paragraph summarizing the history of how toilets were invented.

2. Would you want to own a composting toilet? Why or why not?

3. What is the small hole near the bottom of a toilet bowl called?

    A. the fill valve
    B. the float
    C. the siphon jet

4. What might happen if the flapper got stuck in the open position?

    A. Water would not be able to leave the tank.
    B. Water would run out of the tank until the tank was empty.
    C. Water could not flow over the trap and into the sewer.

Answer key on page 32.

GLOSSARY

chamber pots
Bowls that were used as toilets.

composting
A process involving the natural decay and breakdown of organic material.

conserve
To prevent something from being used up or wasted.

evaporate
To change from a liquid to a gas.

facilities
Buildings or places with a specific use or purpose.

latrines
Outdoor structures, often holes in the ground, that are used as toilets.

sanitation
A system that keeps drinking water safe and removes sewage.

siphon
A curved tube that connects the toilet bowl to the sewer.

siphoning
Using a difference in pressure at the two ends of a curved tube to move a liquid.

TO LEARN MORE

BOOKS

DiPiazza, Francesca Davis. *Remaking the John: The Invention and Reinvention of the Toilet*. Minneapolis: Twenty-First Century Books, 2015.

Marsico, Katie. *Stinky Sanitation Inventions*. Minneapolis: Lerner Publications, 2014.

Yomtov, Nel. *The Grimy, Gross, Unusual History of the Toilet*. Mankato, MN: Capstone Press, 2012.

NOTE TO EDUCATORS

Visit **www.focusreaders.com** to find lesson plans, activities, links, and other resources related to this title.

INDEX

Answer Key: 1. Answers will vary; 2. Answers will vary; 3. C; 4. B